Away in a Manger

DAILY DEVOTIONS

Copyright © 2008 Concordia Publishing House
3558 S. Jefferson Ave., St. Louis, MO 63118-3968
1-800-325-3040 • www.cph.org

Scripture quotations are from The Holy Bible, English Standard Version®. Copyright
© 2001 by Crossway Bibles, a publishing ministry of Good News Publishers, Wheaton,
Illinois. Used by permission. All rights reserved.

Quotations marked AE are from vols. 11, 13, 16, 18 of *Luther's Works*, American Edition,
copyright © 1976, 1956, 1969, 1975 by Concordia Publishing House. All rights reserved.

Hymn texts with the abbreviation *LSB* are from *Lutheran Service Book*, copyright © 2006
by Concordia Publishing House. All rights reserved.

Manufactured in the United States of America

Library of Congress Cataloging-in-Publication Data

Murray, Scott R.
Away in a manger : daily devotions / Scott R. Murray.
        p. cm.
ISBN 978-0-7586-1449-0
1. Advent—Prayers and devotions. 2. Devotional calendars. I. Murray, Scott R. II. Title.
BV4254.5.A93 2008
263'.91—dc22

                                2008012081

1 2 3 4 5 6 7 8 9 10   17 16 15 14 13 12 11 10 09 08

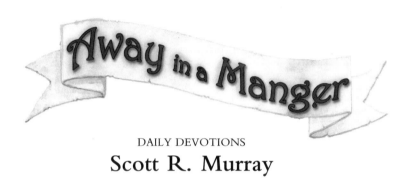

DAILY DEVOTIONS

Scott R. Murray

CONCORDIA PUBLISHING HOUSE • SAINT LOUIS

November 27

God's Little Sign of Life

There shall come forth a shoot from the stump of Jesse,
and a branch from his roots shall bear fruit. (Isaiah 11:1)

History is filled with both great aspiration and great destruction. Destruction is often the cost of selfish ambition, and this was certainly the case when King Sennacherib of Assyria invaded Jerusalem (701 BC), stripping the region of its trees and leaving only stumps. However, we often don't think of this devastation as the work of the Lord of hosts, who brings judgment on His people (Isaiah 10:33–34). But the Lord does not bring destruction without hope. Out of the devastation worked by the Lord's servants sprouted a shoot. The Lord was not going to leave Judah and Jerusalem without a Son from the house of David.

David's tender house arises from the tree devastated at the command of God, though some would say that such a recovery is hardly an impressive comeback. A devastated ruling house needs more than a tender shoot. Tenderness will not hold off the next foreign king intent upon domination. In less than a hundred years, Babylon would become the scourge of Jerusalem in the hands of God, Assyria would be defeated by the eager Babylonians, and the Persians would crush the Babylonians. A shoot appears weak and helpless in the wake of all of this destruction. However, the little house of Jesse stands forever and now reigns in the world through the Church.

The hymn "Away in a Manger" shows us how something weak and helpless can hold immense power. The house of Jesse is restored in the birth of the shoot from the Virgin Mary. The little Lord Jesus bore much fruit through weakness and death on the cross. From that stump of His death comes the fruit of life in our forgiveness of sins. His lowly lordship has the power to undo the domination of the kings on earth.

November 28

The Lord We Need

And the Spirit of the LORD shall rest upon Him,
the Spirit of wisdom and understanding, the Spirit
of counsel and might, the Spirit of knowledge
and the fear of the LORD. (Isaiah 11:2)

Great things are expected of the messianic shoot, a mere babe. How can He accomplish the will of the Lord? He uses the weapons of the Spirit in the Lord's kingdom, though not those we know best, such as guns, bombs, and armies. Instead, He uses the fruit of the Spirit. The divinely given seven-fold gifts of the Spirit are His in fullest measure.

The Lord is the Lord we need because He is not just an infant. The humble, yet perfect weaponry of the Spirit is the Lord's whole arsenal. He has the practical knowledge that applies the right Word of God to comfort and forgive poor sinners like us when we feel our trouble. His understanding makes correct judgments, though they may be divisive, to judge by the truth of His Word. He has the Spirit's counsel as a complete plan of action to save the world.

The Lord is the Lord we need because His might will not be undone in the execution of His plan to justify the wicked. His knowledge of the Father is the deepest possible insight into, and grasp of, His heavenly Father's will. The fear of the Lord is the capstone of His characteristics by which He shows the deepest respect and reverence toward God.

All these characteristics He possesses in His weakness and littleness. Our Messiah has all the gifts of God. As God, He possesses these by nature. As man, He enjoys them through the personal union of the two natures in one Christ. He is an all-powerful Lord who is so little as to be "asleep on the hay," and thus fully one of us. This is the Lord we need.

November 29

The Little Judge

And His delight shall be in the fear of the LORD.
He shall not judge by what His eyes see, or decide
disputes by what His ears hear. (Isaiah 11:3)

How afraid a child standing in an earthly court of law must be. We are all children standing in front of the Lord for judgment. Yet the meekness of our Judge born a child invites all His dear children into His tender care. Our Lord says, "Let the little children come to Me" (Matthew 19:14). The One whose delight is in the fear of the Lord will support the meek and lift up the lowly. He will not judge by external appearances or by who has the best excuses; He will render the verdict of acquittal over those who recognize that they have done nothing to deserve it. The Lord will speak words of peace to those of us who fear that a state of war exists between us and our God; He invites those who will not receive a fair shake from the world to seek His judgment. "The people of Christ's kingdom are the poor, the mean, the insignificant, the faint-hearted, the harassed, the lowly, the fearful. These He will judge; that is, He will make the just cause prevail, He will justify them, He will give them grace, He will forgive the sins of those who acknowledge and confess them and do not rely on themselves" (AE 16:121).

His court invites the children to the judgment rendered by His perfect justice. That judgment is the righteousness of faith. He meekly takes all the children by the hand and tells them they are righteous and have been placed among the righteous. The season of Advent may be said to be a time for children, and so it is. We all become children in the court of the Child King, the little Lord Jesus. He will judge us not by what He sees in us or hears from us but by what He has done.

November 30

Judgment Ends with Jesus

With righteousness He shall judge the poor, and decide
with equity for the meek of the earth; and He shall strike
the earth with the rod of His mouth, and with the breath
of His lips He shall kill the wicked. (Isaiah 11:4)

God's judgment comes with a decisive wrath that strikes and slays. Who upon the earth will not be struck by the rod of His mouth and the breath of His lips? The word that comes forth from His mouth kills the earthly-minded and wicked. God's children also receive the thundering velvet hand of their heavenly Father, but with confidence that the One who kills also makes alive, that He daily slays our sinful flesh and puts to death our old Adam. We confess that such judgment must be a sign of His love for us, just as it was a sign of His love for our Lord Jesus.

A twofold judgment comes in the Word of God. This Word "has power both to save and to destroy. It saves the godly, that is, those who believe and make no claims for themselves, but it destroys the ungodly, that is, those who are proud in their own wisdom and righteousness. But it smites and brings to naught earthly and ungodly men, toward repentance and toward conversion and toward constant enlargement of His reign" (AE 16:121–22). We are ever subject to this twofold judgment unto death and life, repentance and forgiveness. He who looks down from the sky judges us, and His equity forgives us for His own dear sake.

The divine judgment begins and ends with Jesus Himself: "The LORD has laid on Him the iniquity of us all" (Isaiah 53:5). Thus, we can rest in His tender care, even in this season when we see Him as a helpless infant, because He has suffered all that He sends us. He comes to bring both death to the proud old Adam and life to the poor and meek.

December 1

Dressed for Victory

Righteousness shall be the belt of His waist,
and faithfulness the belt of His loins. (Isaiah 11:5)

A United States Marine in full battle dress is an impressive foe. The uniform tells the enemy that defeat is inevitable. The Messiah is likewise dressed for battle; our foes will be defeated by Him. Christ wrestles our enemies into submission, bringing victory to His people. In the ancient world, the flowing robes of a well-dressed warrior were tucked into his belt when he went into action—the wearing of a belt meant that he was going to war. Christ's belt is an indispensable sign of His mission to defeat our enemies. The Messiah's weapons are His righteousness and His faithfulness. These show His actions to be decisive and certain. These are the weapons of God's Son, who, though a child in the manger, is fully equipped to accomplish our salvation and be our Protector. He is no ordinary child. By the union of His divine and His human natures, He is heir to all that the Father has. There is no doubt that He will emerge from the battle with the victory wreath to bestow on us, the recipients of His favor. By the weapon of His faithfulness and righteousness, He has gained the victory:

> All trials are overcome, when we believe that Christ is our Protector, in whom we have all things, even though we are sinners. Such, then, is this kingdom, that first the spoken Word of God is proclaimed and then it is believed, the Holy Spirit being active in both cases. This is the righteousness before God and, as 1 John 5:4 calls it, "the victory that overcomes the world" and all evils. This is the difference between this kingdom and all others, which are physical. (AE 16:122)

So powerful is the Word of His mouth that mere physical kingdoms are not won by Him, but the kingdom counted righteous by the blood He sheds in battle. The Messiah is dressed for victory. Ours.

December 2

When the Little Child Leads

*The wolf shall dwell with the lamb, and the leopard shall lie down
with the young goat, and the calf and the lion and the fattened calf
together; and a little child shall lead them. (Isaiah 11:6)*

Nothing is more delightful than the picture of the Second Adam leading
the wild creatures of Eden now tamed again. The little Child—dwarfed
by the ravenous wolf, the prowling leopard, and the devouring lion—leads
them without fear. Nature run amok, groaning for the redemption now given
by the Child, only slaughters, bringing death as a sign of God's wrath. But
that wrath has been tamed by the little Lord Jesus; He makes peace in the
realm of nature.

The Gospel writers do not write the beasts of the field into their nativ-
ity scene. However, it is not for nothing that the manger is depicted as sur-
rounded by them. The baby who does not cry when the cattle are lowing
is the baby who has made peace between creation and the Creator. All the
brokenness worked by the fall of Adam has been swallowed up by this little
Child. This Child is nature's God.

If this Child can tame the vengeance introduced into nature by the poi-
soning fall, He can certainly tame the wrath of God that oversees this vengeance. He has tamed the beast that rages in the broken heart of every person
since Adam. In this way, nature has been reduced to a petting zoo for the
children of God who follow the little Child and His tamed nature. As God,
the little Child places a lion tamer's power into the Church's hands through
the humble Word of the little Child. "The church will convert the nations
not by force but by the goodness of the Word. The lion will fill himself with
straw and stubble, that is, he will become tame and adopt a domestic gentle-
ness, just as the ox will submit to the hand" (AE 16:123). How different the
world looks when the little Child leads.

December 3

Food of Life

The cow and the bear shall graze; their young shall lie down together; and the lion shall eat straw like the ox. (Isaiah 11:7)

God's Word does not appear appetizing at first. It challenges our self-righteousness and destroys our pious self-image. It tells us the impossible: the little Lord Jesus has accomplished our salvation when we could not. We, who have come of age, cannot work our own way into the good graces of God. How can we swallow that? We feel that the Word needs to be choked down like straw. We wonder why the message cannot be more user-friendly—perhaps juicier and more attractive to us, like the cow to the bear. But the Word of God is none other than the little Lord Jesus Himself. The Word is the very bread that comes down out of heaven at the incarnation, from which perfect peace comes: "And the bread that I will give for the life of the world is My flesh" (John 6:51). Tooth and claw now no longer reign. All alike eat the wheaten food that is Christ. So we neither devour nor are devoured, but are fed on the food of peace.

This food, the Word of God, changes everything. Yes, we know that we humans remain charged with wickedness; however, the savage and wild are tamed by the Word of God and come into the community led by Christ, the little Child: "Human beings differing extremely among themselves—savage, wild, irascible, hateful, murderous, ungovernable, and the people of the gentle Christ—come to agreement through the preaching of the Gospel" (AE 16:122–23). The taming Word of God now provides real nourishment for the world into which Jesus was born among the animals. Although we still see the wildness of fallen humans, there is a pacifying Word of God, which the people of God preach into the wilderness. The little Lord Jesus proclaims forgiveness, the true food of life.

December 4

Nothing to Fear

The nursing child shall play over the hole of the cobra,
and the weaned child shall put his hand
on the adder's den. (Isaiah 11:8)

The little child is so careless of the adder and the cobra. How can He play with these deadly creatures? How can the mother not be alarmed when she notices her child playing with these lethal enemies? There is nothing to fear because they have been defanged by the God who saves those who have fallen into the deadly embrace of the serpent, who, slithering into Eden, brought death. All of God's children can play among these evils because they cannot harm where the Word of God holds sway. Indeed, the mission of the Church's children is to play among the deadly creatures of this world in defiance of all evil. The Church's children can defy the false teaching of the serpent Satan because they have a Child Lord who has defeated these deadly enemies. This is why we celebrate at Advent and Christmas. We celebrate because the birth of the Word of God among us pushes back the ancient darkness. Christmas is the beginning of the end for the old serpent. The Christ Child has placed His hand among these enemies and has not felt their sting. He has swallowed up their poison and pulled their fangs out.

"All who are in Christ are called children, and they enjoy dealing with devils. This, then, is the fruit of the Word, to turn men from every error and tyranny. The little boy pulls the snakes out with his hand, that is, the preacher by means of the spoken Word casts out the devils because the Holy Spirit is present" (AE 16:123). In Christ, we are set free from what we fear and spend our days in confident celebration.

December 5

Freed

They shall not hurt or destroy in all My holy mountain;
for the earth shall be full of the knowledge of the LORD
as the waters cover the sea. (Isaiah 11:9)

The Church is God's holy mountain. In Isaiah's day, Jerusalem hardly fit this description. The city was the scene of power politics, sexual immorality, and oppression of the poor (Isaiah 3:14–15). Jerusalem's inhabitants thought that no harm would befall them because they had God in the container of the temple. He had become for them a talisman of protection. Isaiah was warning that their ignorance of the Lord's good news would fail them in the end because God would not let His presence become a good luck charm to ward off attack. A Child would change God's relationship to His people. All harm would fall upon God's Son, every hurt would be taken up by Him (Isaiah 53), so that those who dwell on the Zion of God would live free from all hurt and harm.

"There will be supreme peace and harmony in Christ's kingdom, and people will neither offend nor destroy one another. They have and make peace. Christians are peacemakers 'among those who hate peace,' as Ps. 120:6 says, yet in such a way that the church is not changed, but the wolves, leopards, lions, and bears are. Those who hold our teaching have peace. The true knowledge of Christ begets harmony" (AE 16:123). Christ has worked harmony among us through the Gospel proclamation. This knowledge will be extensive and deep, like the waters of the sea, and will also cleanse us of our unrighteousness: "By His knowledge shall the righteous one, My servant, make many to be accounted righteous, and He shall bear their iniquities" (Isaiah 53:11). Peace with God is made by Him. Our knowledge of it frees us from all hurt and harm.

December 6

A Sign for the Peoples

In that day the root of Jesse, who shall stand as a signal
for the peoples—of Him shall the nations inquire,
and His resting place shall be glorious. (Isaiah 11:10)

When the great tree in the churchyard was cut down, we thought that was the end of it. However, the next year the stump supported a shoot. The life of the root could not be denied. Isaiah foresaw that the messianic house of Jesse would be cut down, but that its life could not be denied. It would spring up again among the people like us (Romans 15:12). Those who were thought not to be the people of God "in that day" have become My people, says our God.

He has called the Gentiles to rally around the sign that is lifted up. "Christ is called . . . banner and military ensign, that His reign stands up in the daily battle and its attacks; those who serve God are called the army, and God is called God of hosts. Their enemies are Satan, flesh, sins, world, death. And the Gospel is called the Word of the cross in 1 Cor. 1:18" (AE 16:124). Christ said that His crucifixion would attract all people: "And I, when I am lifted up from the earth, will draw all people to Myself" (John 12:32). When lifted up, He would be the sign of the salvation of the world.

Christ's ministry was focused on humiliation and death but ended with the glory of His resurrection. He was raised from His resting place so that the tomb would become gloriously empty, as was foretold. This symbolizes to us that the sorrow and suffering of this life will be followed by a glorious resting place. So the Lord Jesus, resurrected and triumphant, is still a sign of hope for the people marked, as He is, by the wounds that give life.

December 7

Above All

It shall come to pass in the latter days that the mountain
of the house of the LORD shall be established as the highest
of the mountains, and shall be lifted up above the hills;
and all the nations shall flow to it. (Isaiah 2:2)

Advent is a time of waiting, set between the first and second comings of Jesus. Christians wait in the house of the Lord, which the Lord has lifted up above all other mountains. Jerusalem of old was not the tallest mountain in its region. However, the people always ascended Mount Zion, where God dwelt among His people. His dwelling among them is the exaltation of the people of God. In nearness to His perfect presence, God lifts up those who never deserve the presence of God.

Waiting can be tiresome to the faithful. In this present evil age, we await redemption through the Lord who has built the Church and exalted it. We struggle to wait patiently because it is hard to endure in these days of rampant godlessness, manifest evil, and false teaching, even in the Church. Still, we must take solace in the fact that Christ comes to us in His body and blood. Only when the Lord is close enough to be received with our mouths will we have true peace in these latter days, and this is because the Lord's kingdom is stronger than any other: "No matter how much the church is sure to be harassed and trampled underfoot by death, sins, Satan, tyranny, and heretics, yet in this trampling underfoot it shall be exalted above all mountains. For no other kingdom is so firmly established" (AE 16:28). Every other earthly kingdom has fallen or will fall. Yet because God chose to establish His presence among His people in Christ Jesus, we live even now by faith on that hill of the Church lifted above all.

December 8

Draw Us to You

*Many peoples shall come, and say: "Come, let us go up
to the mountain of the LORD, to the house of the God of Jacob,
that He may teach us His ways and that we may walk in
His paths." For out of Zion shall go the law, and the word
of the LORD from Jerusalem. (Isaiah 2:3)*

The Word draws people to Zion. The proclamation of Christ, who is the Word, goes out from the Church, the mountain of the Lord. This proclamation is much different than the voice that rumbled down Mount Sinai, bringing fear and trembling, threatening death (Exodus 19). Sinai's law is not what Isaiah is thinking of here. He is speaking of instruction in the incarnate Word, Jesus. The instruction of the Lord brings salvation to those who belong in the house of Jacob's God.

Isaiah awakens those upon the path of the Lord to their need for the Lord's salvation by reminding them that they are Jacob. Jacob was the old name of Israel, replaced by God (Genesis 32:28). The name Jacob reminds us that we are not worthy of our entry into Zion. Only the true Son of God has the ancient doors opened for Him (Psalm 24:9). The rest of us are Jacob, which means "supplanter." Jacob snatched the birthright from his careless older brother, Esau. Although the Church is named for Jacob, it is still the house of God. The Lord does not abandon spiritual supplanters like us, but makes us His own through the forgiving Word that draws us up to the mountain. The Word makes Jacob new. He becomes a true Israel of God. "By the Word alone, therefore, the church is recognized, and in the glory of the Word the reign of Christ is described. The Word draws the people, makes them willing and joyful" (AE 16:32). The Word of the Lord is still going forth from Jerusalem, drawing the peoples to the mountain of the Lord. O Lord, draw us to You.

December 9

War Obsolete

*He shall judge between the nations, and shall decide disputes
for many peoples; and they shall beat their swords into plowshares,
and their spears into pruning hooks; nation shall not lift up sword
against nation, neither shall they learn war anymore. (Isaiah 2:4)*

Many people think that ultimate peace can be gained by military conflict, but every "war to end all wars" has been followed by another. We all want to "give peace a chance," but that has not worked out very well, and that is because our efforts will never be enough. True peace will ultimately come only from the Prince of Peace, Christ.

Because the Lord Christ grants His righteousness, He is also the One that establishes peace. Certainly, we see and feel the daily conflict of the world, especially in our own hearts. But even in the midst of that sin-driven madness, the Church still has and proclaims peace. The Lord speaks His Word and proclaims that all our warring madness is on the Prince of Peace. By going to the cross, Jesus went to the front line to earn our peace, and thereby, like Uriah, was cut down to cover the wickedness of others (2 Samuel 11).

War exhausts itself upon Christ so that it cannot touch us. If we have the righteousness that comes from Christ, what war can overcome us? If we have the Word of God, it will judge us to be freed from our sins. It will still our hearts and quiet the battle that rages there. When God gathers the nations, war will be no more. There will be nothing to go to war over. We will no longer care for our earthly possessions: "For those who hear and believe this, for what will they contend? If my property, wisdom, and righteousness are of no avail before God, why should I fight it out for them?" (AE 16:32). When the Lord comes to take us to live with Him in His tender care, the art of war will be obsolete.

Light Hidden

O house of Jacob, come, let us walk in the light of the LORD.
(Isaiah 2:5)

Isaiah makes a passionate appeal to the people of Zion. The Lord Himself is the light of the people, so the prophet is calling them into the orbit of His radiance, centered around the temple. The glorious temple of Solomon was not to be dedicated to the legalistic works of grasping Jacob. Instead, the temple was to be where those who recognized the darkness of their own hearts and lives came for illumination, an illumination that calls wickedness by name and shines forgiving beams back into the darkness, piercing it with its brilliance.

The people thought that they had captured Christ in the temple; His presence would be a talisman against trouble. This spiritual darkness, this pride, dimmed the brilliance of the temple built by the messianic forerunner, Solomon. However, the time for casual self-righteousness has an end both for us and for the house of Jacob. We should be humble because glory on earth is transient. Indeed, darkness threatens us all. For the people of Zion, darkness came when the Babylonians destroyed the temple in 587 BC.

Because of the darkness of sin, God chose to put His brilliance in the Child who was born of Mary. Jacob could never have foreseen a descendant of Solomon who would be lying "in a manger, no crib for a bed," or that someone so powerful could be so small (*LSB* 364:1). But the Child's strength is in His humbleness. The manger cradled the One our efforts could never capture. He chose to be among us under the signs of deepest humility. The One most humbled is the Light of the Lord. ✦

December 11

Desert Garden

The wilderness and the dry land shall be glad; the desert shall
rejoice and blossom like the crocus. (Isaiah 35:1)

As late winter in Canada loosened its icy grip, I looked out the window for the first crocus. The crocus pushes its little bud through the remnants of the icy snow of early spring to be the first floral victor over the season of death. How important that daring flower is to the human psyche, weighed down by cabin fever in the dark and dreary days of late winter. That little flower represents hope in rebirth and renewal. Isaiah paints a picture of people on the edge of spiritual despair. Like us, they were in need of the sign of the crocus; they were desperate for any sign of better days. Isaiah paints for them and for us a picture of the impossible: a desert of death turned into a lush floral garden of life.

The people of Zion had once flourished under the care of God, yet they thought they could still improve their status with their own wisdom. But their wisdom only cultivated a desert choked by weeds. The principle fruit became death. Still, God was encouraging His people because He would return once again to cultivate that desert wilderness into His flourishing land full of blossoms. The Lord would come to build His Church in the most unlikely place, turning a land of bleached bones into the home of joy-pursued life. These changes are powerful, yet humble: "The church flourishes inwardly, not in power, in the wisdom of the flesh, in the gleam of splendid works; but it walks along in a simple form, not in ostentatious holiness, and therefore appears to be quite forsaken and without any glitter. Yet there are internal flowers and delights there, but these are not visible, namely, confidence, peace, life, a cheerful conscience, things that are not seen" (AE 16:299). The Lord creates a land of flourishing life out of a barren wasteland. Death's grip is broken.

December 12

Mixed Metaphors

It shall blossom abundantly and rejoice with joy and singing.
The glory of Lebanon shall be given to it, the majesty of Carmel
and Sharon. They shall see the glory of the LORD,
the majesty of our God. (Isaiah 35:2)

Grammar teachers strictly forbid mixed metaphors. However, Isaiah has the blossoming desert singing, though deserts neither rejoice nor sing. The mixed metaphor heightens the drama of the intervention of God who accomplishes the impossible (Luke 18:27). If God waters the desert, it will become a garden. If God writes the music, the wilderness will rejoice and sing. If the Holy Spirit plants, barren lands will become fruitful plains.

Making the impossible happen is always God's way. Our own churches don't always seem to be good examples of holiness, no matter how small or large they may be (1 Corinthians 1:26). Instead, they are full of people who feel they have no reason to rejoice, sing, or blossom (Isaiah 54:1). But God takes the impossible and does it. God's majesty and glory have been brought into the Church by the knowledge of the Lord. This knowledge is why we have reason to rejoice: "The church . . . sees the majesty and glow of God. The disciples are joyful in the Lord alone. For the church boasts only of the knowledge of the Lord" (AE 16:300).

The Lord gives His glory and majesty to His people through His knowledge (Isaiah 53:11). He sees to it that what was once barren has the Word of God sown in it. What was once a wilderness must have God's glory given to it—and God is the giver. God's glory is to undertake the impossible by taking our sins upon Himself in Christ the Lord. What appears only to be a barren wasteland becomes a lush pasture of life freely given. Impossible, you say? If God can make the desert sing, He can certainly give you joy by taking your sins away in Christ, the glory of the Lord.

Hands and Knees Made Strong

Strengthen the weak hands, and make firm the feeble knees.
(Isaiah 35:3)

We have the Lord. Why should we quake with fear? Yet unbelief plagued the people of Judah, fearful of the lurking Assyrians with their seemingly invincible armies. Their hands fell to their sides in anguish and their knees gave way in horror. They acted as though they did not have a God. They need not have feared because they had a God who was the master of the impossible situation, even its architect. He allows the billows to flow over the gunwales. Waves threaten to swamp the ship of life (cf. Matthew 8:23–27). Everyone feels defeated at some time or another when we face the suffering that God permits to come into our lives as a sign of the cross. God has not abandoned us or fallen asleep at the switch; He is forcing us to call upon Him in prayers. We fall to our knees not to cower, but only to pray and, in joyous faith, to await God's always promised rescue. "The inward joy of the spirit fights with the grief of the body exposed to the cross. Therefore the prophet comforts them with exceedingly great consolations" (AE 16:300).

Weak hands are consoled when the strong hand of God intervenes to save those who have despaired waiting for God's gracious intervention (cf. Exodus 13:9). The Child who would come to save stretches out His hands to receive the Assyrian threat nailing Him to the cross. The feeble knees are strengthened unto prayer when the Messiah comes kneeling in holy prayer for those who are suffering for His name's sake. His intercession establishes us on the battlefront to confront the enemies of the Church, but with hands readied by the Word of God and knees made firm because we are certain that the Lord fights for us (Exodus 14:25). No wave of wickedness will ever remove us from the place the Lord has given us at His side.

December 14

Behold Your God

Say to those who have an anxious heart, "Be strong; fear not!
Behold, your God will come with vengeance, with the recompense
of God. He will come and save you." (Isaiah 35:4)

A sudden wave of fear on the battlefield can turn victory into a rout. In 424 BC, at the Battle of Delium, the Athenians attacked their neighbors to the north, the Thebans. The Athenian soldiers, including notable figures such as the philosopher Socrates, were crushing the Thebans. That is, until they were spooked by the unexpected appearance of a few Theban horsemen, perhaps thinking it was the advance of a second army. The Athenians ran in fear, snatching defeat from the jaws of victory and shaking Athenian military confidence to its foundations. Fear can have devastating effects.

Our God tells us not be afraid because He is the God who comes to save. Behold, your God, conceived by the Holy Spirit and born of the Virgin Mary has handed us a victory; He comes with vengeance to slay our enemies, pushing them off the field of battle with overpowering force. Yet it is easy for those with an anxious heart to be dissatisfied with the weak and seemingly late appearances of God's promised rescue. They believe that they must save themselves if they are to be saved. They quiver at a few horsemen on the horizon, thinking that defeat is just over the next hill.

Behold, your God lies in the manger. You need not fear. The Messiah comes for the sole purpose of saving you. He comes not for Himself, but for you! "God first permits people to condemn and persecute His church, as though He were absent, and then He will come very quickly" (AE 16:301). Be still, anxious heart. Your Savior comes with God's reward. The Child of God makes repayment for your sins by taking your fear-riddled nature upon Himself and rescuing it from the slavery to fear.

December 15

Speak Up

*Then the eyes of the blind shall be opened, and the ears
of the deaf unstopped; then shall the lame man leap like a deer,
and the tongue of the mute sing for joy. (Isaiah 35:5–6a)*

My grandmother suffered from macular degeneration, and my grandfather was quite hard of hearing. Whenever they went anywhere together, it was nearly the deaf leading the blind. Blindness and deafness are signs of the fall in human nature. The blind are kept from reading the Word of God and the deaf from hearing it. Debilitation forced my grandparents to be more dependent not just on each other, but especially on God. In faith, they looked forward with eager expectation to God's rescue from their weaknesses.

The Lord Jesus fulfilled this promise in His earthly ministry (Matthew 11:4–6). Taking on our brokenness and weakness by His incarnation, the little Lord Jesus was born into a world of sin, though He was free from its every stain. He cannot help but confront the ravages of sin in His earthly ministry. He opens the eyes of the blind and unstops the ears of the deaf. "This is taken literally with reference to the miracles of Christ and the church, as we read in the last chapter of Mark (16:17, 18), signs that were necessary to confirm the new Word, signs that were added to the glory of the church, signs that are not done physically in the last time of the church" (AE 16:302). This means that a far more troubling blindness, spiritual blindness, is the target of the Lord's Church. A more ruinous deafness Jesus now seeks to unstop through His ministers. These are the greater works of which Jesus speaks (John 14:12). My grandparents' disabilities did not keep them from knowing Christ through His Word. Christ's Church seeks sight for those who will not see and hearing for those who will not hear. The Word of God has the power. When God opens our mouths, all we have to do is "speak up."

December 16

Gardens in the Desert

For waters break forth in the wilderness, and streams in the
desert; the burning sand shall become a pool, and the thirsty
ground springs of water; in the haunt of jackals, where they lie
down, the grass shall become reeds and rushes. (Isaiah 35:6b–7)

An oasis is a miracle of life in the midst of the desert. All around there is nothing but arid wilderness, with the ever-present threat of death in the bone-bleaching sun. Our lives often exhibit the arid emptiness of the burning desert. Our anger rises to scorch those around us. Our hearts become the haunt of jackals, seeking to devour the vulnerable.

Suddenly, when the water runs out and the jackals begin their prowl, the oasis appears on the horizon. There is cooling water gushing from springs creating pools, not just a miserly wadi sometimes offering water and at other times withholding it. God's Gospel gives the abundance that Isaiah described. The Word of the Lord causes miraculous growth, making streams in the desert, slicing through the burning sands of our broken lives, bringing drink to quench the thirst of those hearts. The water is not ours alone, nor the cooling oasis. Its Gospel power leaps across all human social and cultural boundaries. A week of tropical rain changes things, sweeping away homes. How powerful water can be.

So too the Word. The Word of the Lord grows (Acts 12:24) powerfully if we will but preach it. "As a spring flows forth in moistening streams, so this church, which was desert, should gush out in streams of the teachings of the Gospel, always one stream leaping from another into one city and then another, although in the eyes of the world it might seem forever desert" (AE 16:302–3). The Lord's Word will do that for which He sends it (Isaiah 55:10–11), no matter how desolate things appear.

December 17

Highway of Holiness

And a highway shall be there, and it shall be called the
Way of Holiness; the unclean shall not pass over it. It shall
belong to those who walk on the way; even if they are fools,
they shall not go astray. (Isaiah 35:8)

While touring through rural England, I traveled on ancient roadways. The narrow gaps through which two cars had to pass and the wild twist and turns amazed me. The roads of the ancient world were just uncertain paths upon which commerce and kinship had beaten a trail. Isaiah foresaw a highway of interstate proportions and design by which the people of God would be led into the presence of their God. The Way of Holiness led to the temple of Jerusalem. God was present with His people; He wanted them to have access to His atoning presence. It is no wonder that the Magi arrived at Jerusalem and not Bethlehem (Matthew 2:1) while looking for the King.

The Lord Himself calls the way holy because He will call holy all those who tread into His presence upon it (Isaiah 48:2). "The Gospel has a wide road, a smoothed way by means of the completely firm Word in the footsteps of the holy patriarchs who have gone before. This is the royal and holy way" (AE 16:303–4). The walkways into our own churches should be called the holy way because the Gospel preached there makes holy the ones whom the Father draws into His presence.

I felt like a fool when I was lost in England, but no such foolishness is possible when the Lord lays out the road for His holy ones. The Magi got lost on the tortuous road, but the Lord's Word set them again upon the Way of Holiness, and they came to the place where the child was (Matthew 2:9). This teaches us that the road is broad, clearly marked, paved with God's Gospel, so that the pilgrim progresses as the Lord has intended in His gracious will.

December 18

Free Subjects

No lion shall be there, nor shall any ravenous beast come up on it;
they shall not be found there, but the redeemed shall walk there.
(Isaiah 35:9)

The redeemed will stroll comfortably on the way of holiness (Isaiah 35:8). They will fear no enemies, such as false teachers who feed on the lambs of the Church. The true pastors of the way of holiness will be alert for the false teachers and will beat them off with the truth of God's Word, the Word of His lips (Psalm 17:4). This is the sweet liberty given to the redeemed by the Word of God.

> They will walk safely and securely in freedom, because, redeemed by the Word, they cannot be led astray by laws and traditions, but walk in freedom of conscience. You know that Christian liberty is outwardly subject to all men but inwardly it is lord over all things. It can be condemned by no sin, Satan, Law, etc. Thus it has its being in Christ alone. . . . Thus no righteousness, uprightness, etc. will deliver us. Christ alone is our deliverer. This is Christian liberty. (AE 16:305)

Our freedom is created by and remains dependent upon the little Child who, though He subjected Himself to the wicked world, was the most-free person. Here we see a true picture of Christian freedom in Christ: subject as servant of all and subject to none and Lord of all. His free subjection has made us the subjects of His true freedom. The enemies of Christ may seek to devour us, but Christ has freed us so that we may seek to serve them in our outward life. However, we are truly free like Christ while walking on the way that is guarded by Him.

December 19

Ransomed with the Blood

*And the ransomed of the LORD shall return and come to Zion
with singing; everlasting joy shall be upon their heads; they shall
obtain gladness and joy, and sorrow and sighing shall flee away.
(Isaiah 35:10)*

The seasons of Advent and Christmas are full of singing. Some of the most sublime music ever written celebrates the incarnation of Christ. We come to the Zion of the Church with a joyous song on our hearts. Our joy shall be everlasting because our flesh has been made new in the man-gered Child; there is nothing to sorrow over and nothing to sigh about. He has freely exchanged Himself for us, paying a complete ransom for wicked humans (Romans 4:5), making new our flesh in His own. His life was given as a ransom—making us the ransomed of the Lord.

To ransom means to pay the price. And the price paid for us was great: "But we have been purchased by the Lord, and at great cost we are the redeemed of the Lord, not with gold and silver, but with His precious blood" (AE 16:305). Our ransom has been paid in full, so we can never return to the meandering way of life. Instead, we must wait upon the Lord (Psalm 27:14) and receive from Him His ransom in Christ. This is the passivity of faith, and our passivity is made possible by His activity. While we await His second coming, He is doing what is necessary to bring the ages to their conclusion. We await His second coming because He has done all in His first coming to pay the full ransom for us.

So, during Advent and Christmas we sing to glorify the little Lord Jesus who has ransomed up with the blood that He pours out for us. That singing arises from deep within us because we love this Lord Jesus who promises to stay with us until He takes us to heaven to live with Him there.

December 20

In His Light We See Light

The people who walked in darkness have seen a great light; those
who dwelt in a land of deep darkness, on them has light shined.
(Isaiah 9:2)

We seldom experience complete darkness. Stars, streetlights, and the moon all shine a silver luminescence over the nightscape. Complete darkness would unhinge us and set us to crawling about for enlightenment. Such was the deep darkness felt by those who fell into sin and depravity. They had fallen into the darkened bog of their own sinful filth. Darkness fell on those who had suffered the ravages of the Assyrian hordes casting up sun-blotting dust into the Galilean sky. But, like all hardship, their suffering only pointed to the deeper problem of personal sin. The unhinging darkness resides within, making all people crawl for enlightenment.

And the Holy Spirit gives us this enlightenment: "The people of the whole world, Jews as well as Gentiles, were in darkness, that is, in error, unrighteousness, notions, a false understanding of the Law, etc. *Light* is the Gospel, the gift of the Holy Spirit" (AE 16:97). The Lord Jesus will not leave the people of the world in darkness or under the shadow of death (Matthew 4:12–17), for He is the Light of the world (John 8:12). He goes to Galilee to pronounce the darkness ended and to call the people to repentance.

He calls us, too, through the Word of God. We need to deny the darkness within that He might come among us with the Light. He comes to haul us out of the cesspool of our sin and filth. The enlightening Gospel still brings the Light to us and gives us the gift of the Holy Spirit, with the forgiveness of sins and all His blessings. The Light continues to shine where the One who is the Light of the world is taught and proclaimed, for in His Light we see light (Psalm 36:9).

December 21

A Joyful Noise

You have multiplied the nation; You have increased its joy;
they rejoice before You as with joy at the harvest,
as they are glad when they divide the spoil. (Isaiah 9:3)

We quietly tiptoe around newborns for fear that we will disturb their slumber. Because Christmas includes the birth of the Baby, the cradle-song "Away in a Manger" has that same hushed mood. However, babies normally sleep through lots of noise, awakened only by hunger or wet diapers. But Jesus is no ordinary baby. The baby we welcome in this season is a Lord God who neither slumbers nor sleeps (Psalm 121:4). Therefore, the Christmas season should be more about rejoicing than caution. There is a joyful noise to be made (Psalm 95:1) by the people of God this time of year. This Child, the Son of God, was born of the Virgin to draw all to Himself. He grows a people by building a Kingdom for which He offers Himself unto death and rises to reign over it.

We have become the people of God because we have been adopted as sons of God through the Son. And, if you have had the privilege of watching the oath of citizenship administered, you have experienced a small taste of the joy that is felt when the nation is enlarged. With what exultant joy new citizens respond when they are adopted into their new country! So, too, we should rejoice as all that He has done and earned in His warfare on our account has been given to us. The gladness of Christmas comes because the spoils of His work have been given by the Child to us: "Now Mother Church distributes these spoils and ordains them for various divine services, each one according to his peculiar gifts—some for prophecy, others for teaching, others for administrative duties, others for general service to the poor" (AE 13:14). These spoils should cause us not to pause but to make a joyful noise.

December 22

Contrary to All Expectation

For the yoke of his burden, and the staff for his shoulder,
the rod of his oppressor, You have broken as on the day of Midian.
(Isaiah 9:4)

Israel had fallen on hard times. She was unfaithful to the covenant of grace that God had made with her when He rescued her from oppression in Egypt. Oppressed now by the plundering Midianites, the people of Israel lived in caves, hiding whatever food they managed to produce. Contrary to all expectation, it took just three hundred warriors led by Gideon to inflict a stunning defeat upon the Midianites (Judges 6–8), ending the oppression into which Israel had descended. God demanded that weakness bring victory (Judges 7:2), so that His strength might be seen to triumph. The "day of Midian" became like a victory of weakness over strength. God sent the Baby of Promise to triumph over the old oppressing foes of slavery to the fear of death and the power of sin. The weakest One broke that hideous strength, so that God's strength is made perfect in weakness.

That victory becomes absolute in the Christ Child again. "A child produces this victory, that is, one who is humble by faith in Christ. But this strength has weakness as a prerequisite. Nor is the strength of God in us, unless we first are weak. Thence we as children are victors, not that our smallness conquers, but the strength which is in our weakness and smallness, it does the works (2 Cor. 12:9)" (AE 11:363–64). The littleness of the Baby should give us no reason to wonder about the success of our cause. Victory is all the more certain because weakness is the form of victory that God has chosen not just for Him, but for us all. Contrary to all expectation, the weakness of the Church and her children confirms God's great victory in the Baby.

December 23

Total Disarmament

For every boot of the tramping warrior in battle tumult
and every garment rolled in blood will be burned as fuel
for the fire. (Isaiah 9:5)

The people of Jerusalem saw an enormous Assyrian army invade the city in 701 BC. They watched in disbelief as thousands were left dead on the ground when the Lord fought for Judah. In the aftermath, bodies, boots, bloody garments, the very tools of war were thrown into huge cleansing fires. These fires were set outside the city as symbols of God's victory for Judah and King Hezekiah (2 Kings 19). When these words were published by Isaiah, this was fresh in the minds of the people of God. God had brought peace by stopping war and using battle gear as fuel for the fire.

Whether they are the cleansing flame of fire or a white flag, signs of peace evoke powerful memories for those who have been oppressed by foreign invaders. One of the most powerful images from the end of the Second World War was the *Life* magazine photograph of the nurse swept up in the kiss of a sailor on a New York street on V-J Day in 1945. That photo showed the relief from the fear of death and the optimism about the future that arises only in people who have had a great burden lifted from them. Christians feel this same kind of relief because we have a Lord who fights for us and brings us peace: "There will be no war and human carnage, but love, peace, concord. The Holy Spirit will swallow up those evils with the fire of love, so that they will not be called back, because what fire consumes is reduced to nothing" (AE 16:99). The war with God is over. Our warring madness and the tools of our own destruction have been consumed by the fire of the Lord's love for us, and this assures perfect peace with Him. Total disarmament is possible only with God through His Word. The little Child brings peace.

December 24

For Us

For to us a child is born, to us a son is given;
and the government shall be upon His shoulder,
and His name shall be called Wonderful Counselor,
Mighty God, Everlasting Father, Prince of Peace. (Isaiah 9:6)

" All these words are strong and intense. Above [Isaiah] spoke of the greatest affliction, of darkness and the shadow of death. Likewise of the Law, of sin, and of death, the most oppressive tyrants [6:1-2]. Against them he now places the King born and given to us, who is to set us free from them and implant us into His peaceful and happy reign" (AE 16:100). Everything comes down to the Child born for us and the Son given to us. In human government child-rulers are a plague (Isaiah 3:4). But this Child is no ordinary infant, no terrible ruler puffed up by pride before maturing. No, this is the Son of God, who has a Name above every name (Philippians 2:9–10), yet deigns that He should be born for us and given to us. All He does, He does for our good and salvation. His Father placed all upon His shoulders for our good. He takes up the burden of governing us with the Word and Gospel.

In that Word and Gospel His name is bestowed on His people through the triune outflow from the font of life. He who is the Wonderful Counselor brings us into His royal cabinet in the Church as His counselors gathered around His throne. He who is the Mighty God sets right the weakness of His people triumphing mightily for them over their sin and death. He who is Everlasting Father cares for His people as a loving father cares for his own children. He who is Prince of Peace crowns His subjects with the peace that comes from His justifying work (Romans 5:1). His government of the Church has no other goal than the good of those who are in it. The Child comes for no other reason than "for us."

December 25

Confessing the Child

Of the increase of His government and of peace there will be no end, on the throne of David and over His kingdom, to establish it and to uphold it with justice and with righteousness from this time forth and forevermore. The zeal of the LORD of hosts will do this.
(Isaiah 9:7)

The humility of the Kingdom and its Lord leads the world to think the Church is easy to kill. This is how we come to be among the blessed faithful who are persecuted like the prophets before us (Mathew 5:11). Yet, Christ's kingdom grows exponentially. Persecution and suffering should not cause us to despair, because we have a Lord who seeks the increase of His government.

Although Christ is on David's throne and over David's kingdom, He makes David's kingdom look puny and weak by comparison. The Lord's kingdom has no end; it is established by the Lord's zeal, which is His burning desire to accomplish the salvation of the world. In that zeal He provides the world with a righteousness accomplished by Him and given to every person in His kingdom. "Christ is indeed a King different from David, and the government of His kingdom is different, and yet it is a reign over the same people. To believe in life everlasting is the last article and the greatest. However, Christ prepares, establishes, and strengthens this kingdom in the world through the Word and faith, and He does this in a hidden way" (AE 16:102).

To Herod and everyone of his kind, the little Lord Jesus appears easily snuffed out of existence. But the little Child in the manger is the Lord of hosts who commands angelic armies (Matthew 26:53). He does this not to circumvent suffering but to serve us Christians in our hour of need so that we might confess Him as our Davidic King who saves by His zeal.